DEBT CRASHED

MASTER THE ART OF DEBT MANAGEMENT AND FREEDOM

Lawrence J. Mack

Table of contents

INTRODUCTION

Money is anything or verifiable record that is usually accepted as payment for goods and services and repayment of obligations, such as taxes, in a specific nation or socio-economic setting. The major purposes of money are characterized as a medium of exchange, a unit of account, a store of value, and occasionally, a standard of postponed payment. Anything or verifiable document that meets these functions may be viewed as money.
Money is historically an emerging market phenomenon creating commodity money, although practically all modern money systems are based on fiat money.

Fiat money, like any check or note of debt, is without utility value as a tangible commodity. It obtains its value by being proclaimed by a government to be legal tender; that is, it must be recognized as a means of payment within the limits of the nation, for "all debts, public and private". Counterfeit money may cause good money to lose its worth.
The money supply of a nation consists of currency (banknotes and coins) and, depending on the precise definition used, one or more forms of bank money (the balances held in checking accounts, savings accounts, and other sorts of bank accounts) (the balances held in checking accounts, savings accounts, and other types of bank accounts). Bank money, which consists mainly of records (primarily computerized in contemporary banking), constitutes by far the greatest component of broad money in industrialized nations
The term money stems from the Latin word moneta with the meaning "coin" through French Monnaie. The Latin name is supposed to stem from a temple of Juno, on Capitoline, one of Rome's seven hills. In the ancient world, Juno was commonly connected with money. The temple of Juno Moneta in Rome was the spot where the mint of Ancient Rome was housed. The name "Juno" may have arisen from the Etruscan goddess Uni (which means "the one", "unique", "unit", "union", "unified") and "Moneta" possibly from the Latin word "money" (remind, warn, or teach) or the Greek word "money" (alone, unique) (alone, unique).

Medium of exchange

When money is used to intermediary the exchange of goods and services, it is fulfilling a role as a medium of exchange. It so avoids the inefficiencies of a barter system, such as the inability to permanently secure "coincidence of desires". For example, between two parties in a barter system, one side may not have or create the thing that the other wants, demonstrating the non-existence of the coincidence of desires. Having a means of exchange helps relieve this difficulty since the former can have the flexibility to spend time on other products, instead of being burdened to exclusively service the demands of the latter. Meanwhile, the latter may utilize the medium of trade to hunt for a party that can offer them the thing they desire.

Measure of value

A unit of account (in economics) is a standard numerical monetary unit of measurement of the market worth of commodities, services, and other transactions. Also called a "measure" or "standard" of relative value and delayed payment, a unit of account is a required requirement for the structuring of commercial agreements that entail debt.
Money works as a standard measure and a common currency of commerce. It is therefore a foundation for quoting and haggling of pricing. It is crucial for building effective accounting systems.

Standard of postponed payment

While the standard of postponed payment is distinguished by certain writings, particularly older ones, other texts incorporate this under other functions.
A "standard of delayed payment" is an acceptable mechanism to settle a debt - a unit in which debts are denominated, and the status of money as legal currency, in those countries that have this idea, says that it may function for the discharge of obligations. When obligations are denominated in money, the actual value of loans may vary owing to inflation and deflation, especially for sovereign and international debts through debasement and devaluation.

Money supply

In economics, money is any financial instrument that can satisfy the functions of money. These financial instruments combined are usually referred to as the money supply of an economy. In other terms, the money supply is the number of financial instruments inside a certain economy accessible for buying commodities or services. Since the money supply comprises multiple financial instruments (typically currency, demand deposits, and several other forms of deposits), the quantity of money in an economy is measured by adding up these financial instruments generating a monetary aggregate.

Economists adopt numerous approaches to quantify the stock of money or money supply, expressed in different forms of monetary aggregates, employing a categorization system that relies on the liquidity of the financial instrument employed as money. The most regularly utilized monetary aggregates (or forms of money) are generally called M1, M2, and M3. These are increasingly bigger aggregate categories: M1 is cash (coins and banknotes) plus demand deposits (such as checking accounts); M2 is M1 plus savings accounts and time deposits under $100,000; M3 is M2 plus bigger time deposits and equivalent institutional accounts. M1 comprises just the most liquid financial products and M3 is somewhat illiquid. The specific definitions of M1, M2, etc. may be different in various nations.

Another measure of money, M0, is also used; unlike the other measurements, it does not reflect real buying power by enterprises and consumers in the economy. M0 is the basic money amount of money issued by the central bank of a nation. It is assessed as currency plus deposits of banks and other institutions at the central bank. M0 is also the only money that can meet the reserve requirements of commercial banks.

Creation of money

In modern economic systems, money is generated by two procedures:
Legal tender or narrow money (M0) is the currency issued by a Central Bank by minting coins and issuing banknotes.
Bank money or wide money (M1/M2) is the money generated by private banks via the recording of loans as deposits of borrowing customers, with partial support represented by the cash ratio. Currently, bank money is produced as electronic money.
In most nations, the bulk of the money is largely produced as M1/M2 by commercial banks issuing loans. Contrary to certain common misunderstandings, banks do not serve merely as middlemen, lending out deposits that savers put with them, and do not depend on central bank money (M0) to make new loans and deposits

CHAPTER ONE

DEBT CONSOLIDATION

Even if you're working hard to manage your money the proper way, paying off high-interest debt every month might make it impossible to meet your financial objectives. No matter how much you owe, it might take months or even years to get out of debt.
One approach to cope with several debt payments is by consolidating. Debt consolidation is a kind of money management where you pay off previous obligations by taking out one new loan, commonly via a debt consolidation loan, a balance transfer credit card, student loan refinancing, a home equity loan, or a HELOC.

What is Debt Consolidation ?

Obligation consolidation is the process of integrating various debts into a single debt. Instead of making individual payments to several credit card issuers or lenders each month, you roll them into one payment from a single lender, preferably at a cheaper interest rate. You may use debt consolidation to integrate numerous forms of debt, including:

- Auto loans
- Credit cards
- Medical debt
- Payday loans
- Personal loans
- Student loans

While debt consolidation won't wipe off your total, the technique may make it simpler and less costly to pay off debt. If you acquire a low-interest rate, you might save hundreds or even thousands of dollars in interest. Managing one payment might also make it simpler to keep on top of your obligations and prevent late payments, which can affect your credit.

Types Of Debt Consolidation

No matter what form of debt you're combining, if you're searching for how to consolidate debt, you have a few alternatives to pick from.

- Debt Consolidation Loan

Debt consolidation loans are personal loans that combine numerous debts into one set monthly payment. Debt consolidation loans normally have periods between one and 10 years, and many will allow you to combine up to $50,000.

Most lenders do not stipulate how the loan funds may be utilized. So, it's up to the borrower to apply the loan proceeds to the outstanding credit card and loan amounts they wish to combine. You'll also begin making monthly payments to the new lender for the term of the loan.

Ideally, you want to concentrate on the loans with the highest interest rates first. Also, this choice only makes sense if your new loan's interest rate is lower than the interest rates of your old credit card or loan products. While you might acquire a more reasonable monthly payment if the lender extends the loan term, you'll still spend significantly more in interest by combining.

Best for: Borrowers who seek a more simplified payback method.

- Balance Transfer Credit Card

If you have many credit card obligations, a balance transfer credit card might help you pay down your debt and decrease your interest rate. Like a debt consolidation loan, a balance transfer credit card transfers various streams of high-interest credit card debt onto one credit card with a reduced interest rate.

Most debt transfer credit cards provide a 0 percent APR introductory period, often lasting anywhere from 12 to 21 months. If you can manage to pay off all or most of your debt within the introductory term, you might save thousands of dollars in interest payments.

However, if you have a big outstanding sum once the term is finished, you may find yourself in greater debt in the future, since balance transfer credit cards tend to have higher interest rates than other kinds of debt consolidation.

Best for: Borrowers who can afford to pay off credit cards rapidly.

- Student Loan Refinancing

If you have high-interest student loan debt, refinancing your student loans might help you receive a reduced interest rate. Student loan refinancing enables consumers to combine both federal and private student loans under one fixed monthly payment and better terms.

While refinancing might be a wonderful method to combine your student loans, you'll still have to fulfill eligibility standards. Also, if you refinance federal student loans, you'll lose government

protections and perks, such as income-driven repayment, and deferral possibilities.
Best for: Borrowers with high-interest private student loans.

- Home Equity Loan

A home equity loan — commonly referred to as a second mortgage — allows you to tap into your house's existing equity. Most home equity loans come with payback lengths between five and 30 years, and you may normally borrow up to 85 percent of your property's worth, less any existing mortgage obligations.
Property equity loans tend to offer lower interest rates than credit cards and personal loans because they're secured by your home. The negative is that your house is in danger of foreclosure if you fail on the loan.
Best for: Borrowers with high-interest private student loans.

- Home Equity Line Of Credit

A home equity line of credit (HELOC) is a home equity loan that functions as a revolving line of credit. Like a credit card, a HELOC enables you to withdraw cash as required at a variable interest rate. A HELOC also draws into your house's current equity, so the amount that you may borrow is contingent on the equity you have in your property.
A HELOC is a long-term loan, with the typical draw period — the period when you may access cash — lasting 10 years. The payback term might continue up to 20 years, during which time you can no longer draw from your credit line.
Best for: Borrowers with large me equity who desire an extended payback term.

How To Consolidate Your Debt

If you're attempting to find out how to combine debt, the procedure is quite similar no matter which kind of debt consolidation you are employing. It's crucial to recognize that debt consolidation is distinct from debt settlement. With debt consolidation, you will utilize the proceeds from your new debt consolidation loan to pay off all of your current bills in full.

Once you've acquired the cash from your loan, home equity line of credit, or other debt. Consolidation loan, you may start the debt consolidation procedure. Use those monies to pay off all of your existing debts. Then you will have just one monthly loan payment, often at a lower interest rate than all of the interest rates on your prior loans.

Debt consolidation pros and disadvantages

Debt consolidation isn't the best solution for everyone; before combining your debt, evaluate the advantages and downsides.

Pros

Credit score enhancement. You might notice a credit score rise if you consolidate your debt. Paying off credit cards with a debt consolidation might lessen your credit usage ratio, and your payment history could improve if a debt consolidation loan helps you make more on-time payments.

Less overall interest. If you can combine numerous loans with double-digit interest rates into a single loan with an interest rate below 10 percent, you may save hundreds of dollars on your loan.

Simpler debt payback method. It might be challenging to keep track of many credit cards or loan payments each month, particularly if they're due on various days. Taking one debt consolidation loan makes it easy to organize your month and keep on top of payments.

Cons

Collateral at danger. If you employ any form of secured loan to secure your debt, such as a home equity loan or HELOC, that collateral is liable to seizure should you fall behind on payments.

The higher probable cost of debt. Your potential for savings with a debt consolidation loan relies mainly on how your loan is structured. If you have the same interest rate but pick a longer payback timetable, for instance, you will eventually pay more in interest over time

.

Upfront charges. Any method of debt consolidation might come with expenses, including origination fees, balance transfer fees, or closing charges. You'll want to evaluate these costs with any possible savings before applying.

How to assess whether debt consolidation is best for you

Debt consolidation makes the most sense if your spending is under control and your credit score is high enough to qualify for a more competitive interest rate than you're now paying. You should also evaluate your present debt burden while choosing whether debt consolidation is good for you. If it's manageable, doesn't take up an excessive amount of your monthly gross income, and will take more than a few months to pay off, consolidating your debt could be a smart financial move.

When Not To Consolidate Debt

Debt consolidation is only successful if you're disciplined enough to cease using the credit cards you pay off. Otherwise, you risk collecting significantly more debt than you began with. It's equally crucial to guarantee you can afford the amount of the monthly payment on the debt consolidation loan. If the payment spreads your budget too thin, you might fall behind quite fast and harm your credit rating.

Also, evaluate your credit rating before you decide to combine debt. If your credit score is on the lower end, the lender or creditor would likely only offer harsher interest rates to assist you to consolidate what you owe.

CHAPTER TWO

DEBT'S EFFECTS ON YOUR LIFE

Many Americans have struggled with debt for a long time, but the extraordinary issues of the last three years have affected tens of millions more people. Our lives have undergone significant change as a result of the COVID-19 epidemic and its aftermath, including in the areas of our health, employment, and financial stability.

More lately, rising inflation, skyrocketing gas costs, and even shortages of infant formula have added misery to the crisis to uncertainty.

Problems are being caused by more than simply a shortage of money. A severe lack of funds resulted in a sharp rise in denial, tension, rage, sadness, and anxiety. The stress of dealing with debt may be almost as detrimental emotionally as having your power shut off, having your vehicle repossessed, or having your credit score fall to the point where it will be difficult for you to get another loan.

According to a Federal Reserve Bank of Philadelphia analysis from 2021, 2 million families owe nearly $15 billion in late rent alone on housing. According to a National Equity Atlas research, such an amount is more than $21 billion.

Regardless of the price or the reason, debt causes mental devastation in our minds. Low self-esteem and cognitive decline are some of the negative impacts. That implies that when you're stressed out because you can't pay your water bill, you won't be as able to study, remember, pay attention, or solve issues.

And get this: **Debt can be painful. I mean, it hurt a lot.**

That wasn't all that shocking, but a study team found that even just contemplating the possibility of financial uncertainty was enough to make the pain worse. Compared to those who thought about a secure moment in their lives, people reported experiencing nearly twice as much bodily discomfort after remembering an insecure financial phase in their lives.

It's uncommon for someone to live without financial issues. Jobs go, relationships end in divorce, individuals grow ill, their houses lose value, and the expenses simply keep coming in. Particularly during and after a pandemic, nobody is immune.

Therefore, which came first—the suffering or the debt?

Mental Health and Debt

Does mental illness cause debt, or does debt create mental disease?

Yes .

After many years of investigation, it is the best response that can be offered. According to some studies, stress from financial anxiety weakens your resistance to mental health issues.

According to other research, mental health issues erode self-control, increase expenditure, and generally impair one's ability to make sound financial decisions. That might explain why Jack Nicholson in "One Flew Over the Cuckoo's Nest" didn't have a bank account.

There are numerous different problems and levels of severity that fall under the umbrella of "mental illness." Whether it is a little problem that seems to be going away or a serious, persistent one, it is crucial to be aware of it, recognize it, and take action to solve it.

Behavior patterns that encourage certain people to spend recklessly may lead to debt just as easily as a financial emergency brought on by a car accident. Regardless of how one becomes behind on their payments, being in debt may cause uncomfortable emotional reactions.

The most basic aspects of our financial life may be the source of many of these behavioral habits. As they come to terms with the fact that they cannot repay their student debts or may have to default on them, the majority of student loan borrowers report a decline in mental health and rising worry.

DENIAL

Washington D.C. has always been known for its culture of denial, but as a result of the COVID-19 relief laws and the subsequent inflation problem, the flow has exploded into a torrent.

In 2022, the national debt reached $30 trillion. The Congressional Budget Office forecasted an additional $1 trillion increase in the budget deficit for 2022.

Although many behave as though they do, consumers don't have the luxury of unlimited deficit spending. They ignore their declining financial situation while engaging in excessive spending. They put off solving issues until a third party, such as being refused credit, facing foreclosure, being sued, or receiving harassing phone calls from debt collectors, forces a change.

The following are a few signs of debt denial:

- Minimizing the amount you owe.
- Whenever you believe a collection agency is calling, don't answer the phone.
- Storing cash in a drawer or leaving it unsealed.
- When your current credit card is maxed out, get a new one.

reassuring yourself that everyone is experiencing the same thing.

Such actions just result in greater debt as interest and late fees mount. However, the brain's helpful protection strategy is to ignore reality. It serves to defend your ego and serve to justify errors. The issue is that reality inevitably sets in.

Stress

It's the reverse of denial, and according to data on debt management, there's a lot of it. Stress and debt are similar to conjoined twins. According to a 2022 survey by Lending Tree, the average credit card debt for American families is $6,569 per person.

Throughout approximately 506 million credit card accounts, Americans owe $841 billion in total.

According to the study, the likelihood that a borrower would report having problems paying monthly obligations rises by 65% for every $10,000 in credit card debt. They were 50% more likely to disclose continuing financial issues.

Consumers who have credit card debt indicated it had an impact on their overall satisfaction to the tune of 40%. One in five people claimed it hurt their health, and one-third said it hurt their level of life.

Unfavorable behavioral changes might result from stress. That holds for all types of stress, including financial stress. Debt-related stress may cause chronic stress, which raises the risk of drug and alcohol dependence and the likelihood of suicide. According to research published in 2021 in the American Journal of Epidemiology, persons experiencing severe financial stress are 20 times more likely to attempt suicide.

What is "STRESS" then?

Endocrinologist Hans Selye first used the phrase in 1936 and described it as "the non-specific reaction of the organism to any need for change."

Larger issues like your employment may be affected since you worry that losing it might worsen your financial condition. It may have an impact on little things like lunch when you feel bad for buying an iced tea instead of water for $2.19. That's no way to live, and you don't need an endocrinologist to tell you that.

Anxiety

The scab on the wound of tension has been ripped off. Not only do you feel uneasy when you imagine receiving a late payment notice, but you also experience a quick pulse, shortness of breath, dry mouth, a headache, and shivers.

Additionally, debt provides hesitant individuals with one more excuse not to go down the aisle of marriage. High levels of debt, according to University of Wisconsin researchers, are a factor in the decline of marriage among young people.

Additionally, people's financial issues persisted after getting married. According to a 2021 CNBC study, 54% of Americans believed that debt was a factor in divorce. Although financial issues were not "the most significant cause of divorce," they "raised stress and tension inside the marriage."

Similarly, a 2019 study published in the Journal of Family and Economic Issues indicated that the likelihood of financial anxiety increased by 6% for every $1,000 in extra student loan debt and by 4% for every $1,000 in additional credit card debt.

Sleepless nights may be attributed to the average student loan debt of $37,014 in 2022.

40 million Americans, according to the National Institute of Mental Health, experience anxiety. An enormous cause of such diseases is financial anxiety.

You anticipate the worse, such as that you'll lose your home if it goes into foreclosure or that your vehicle will break down on the way to work and you'll be fired for being late.

Nobody wants to live in such a way.

Additionally, they reportedly do not want to marry somebody who lives in such a manner.

Anger

Anger problems increase when the economy struggles. Debt-Anger Syndrome is the term used in medical circles to describe the phenomenon.

Victims get angry rather than panicking or denying their difficulties. They are enraged with their creditors for sending them invoices regularly, the mailman for delivering the bills, their employers for not paying them more, their wives for not earning more money,

their children for requiring new braces, and themselves for putting themselves into this situation.
Simply put, they hate life.
Relationships may be ruined, but the physiological impacts can also include heart disease, migraines, and lowered infection resistance.
Surprisingly, suicide rates decreased during the epidemic. In 2020, fewer Americans committed suicide, according to the Centers for Disease Control. The yearly decline was the biggest in over 40 years.
Given that overall mental-health difficulties increased dramatically as a result of the shutdown, researchers are unsure of what caused the welcome drop. They hypothesize that better access to treatment and a shift in public opinion about suicide were factors.
Since so many individuals were experiencing emotional pain, getting medical care became less stigmatized. That implies that self-awareness is the first stage. If you're having financial problems, know that you're not alone and be aware of the potential effects it may have on your health, disposition, and general well-being. It's normal to ask for assistance from mental health specialists just as it is from financial experts.

Depression

Debt causes people to deny, panic, and act out. Even after they complete those steps, the bills are still in their direct line of sight. Depression then begins to set in.
Amid the epidemic, it spread like a virus. According to a 2020 Kaiser Family Foundation (KFF), Health Tracking Poll, families who experienced a loss of income or employment had at least one negative impact on their mental health. This includes problems with eating or sleeping, a rise in alcohol or drug usage, and a worsening of chronic diseases.
Low self-esteem and hopelessness develop. Since those who experience depression sometimes attempt to treat themselves to shopping sprees or other forms of mental escape, this might result

in even greater debt. Depression has the opposite impact of what is intended—it encourages impulsive expenditure.

But all it does is increase debt, which increases dejection and hopelessness. People stop caring whether their misery is brought on by debt or if the debt is causing their agony at that moment.

They want the suffering to stop.

The Impact of Debt on Physical Health

Your physical and emotional wellness are interconnected. The two overlap and have both positive and negative effects on one another.

The results are seldom favorable when stress and debt are present.

Your physical health may be negatively impacted by debt and stress in a variety of ways, including but not limited to:

Blood pressure is impacted by both food and general health. When stress is added, this may become very bad.

The rhythms of your heart may be impacted by your heart rate, which in turn can cause stroke and other occurrences.

Immune system processes have received a lot of attention in the media throughout the epidemic.

The mood has both internal (such as on your mental health) and exterior effects (such as your important relationships).

Memory loss, may affect it and thus increase stress.

Gaining or losing weight might have an impact on blood pressure and heart health.

DEBT'S NEGATIVE EFFECTS ON YOUNG ADULTS

No matter their age, color, level of education, or financial means, debt is ready to plague anybody. However, how each of those groups approaches debt and the problems that come with it varies.

For young people, who increasingly start their adult life with heavy student loan debt that impacts every area of their lives, these difficulties are particularly intimidating. These distinct difficulties result in distinct amounts and types of stress.

The research highlighted the effect of debt and financial hardship on the mental health of persons between the ages of 18 and 24. The survey's limits were designated by those ages, although there is no absolute cutoff age of 25. Lesson: Early debt responsibilities result in early problems to manage debt, both financially and psychologically.

According to the analysis,

- 24 percent of those polled said they had already run into financial trouble and debt.
- Among them, 81 percent said that debt had a detrimental impact on their mental health.
- 31 percent have looked for mental health assistance.
- 84 percent of people express overall worry about the future.
- 69 % are concerned about delinquent debts.

Even if there are no simple answers to these problems, they must be dealt with. Young people may navigate the deeper, rougher waters ahead by developing a healthy, proactive plan for dealing with financial issues before they get out of control.

DEBT'S HARMFUL EFFECTS ON OLDER ADULTS

Younger individuals have stressed their early financial obligations, such as education loans and auto payments, while the older age has its own unique set of urgent problems.

Mortgages, credit cards, and personal debts that have accrued over decades of living may put persons nearing retirement age or even those seeking to make retirement plans in a predicament.

Debt inhibits discipline and temperance, which are two qualities that are normally necessary for retirement savings. Prioritizing retirement savings above debt repayment might be challenging when there is a lot of debt. Simply, seniors have fewer alternatives for financial aid.

According to a 2018 study by the Consumer Bankruptcy Project titled "The Graying of U.S. Bankruptcy," Americans over 65 are filing for bankruptcy at an alarmingly high rate due to the deterioration of the social safety net, which includes Social Security and Medicare, as well as rising healthcare, prescription drug, and other expenses.

The proportion of older citizens declaring bankruptcy increased by more than 500% between 1991 and 2018. These figures might become much more concerning if Florida Senator Rick Scott pushes for the repeal of Social Security.

CHAPTER THREE

MANAGING FINANCIAL STRESS & DEBT

The optimum method to cope with debt-related stress is to prevent it. While it seems impracticable, there are methods to manage stress by creating tactics and financial habits that help minimize both debt and stress:

- Writing down debt: To effectively resolve your debt, it helps to recognize when you have too much debt.
- Identifying your debt: Once you generate a list, evaluate it. You need to recognize which debts are unsecured and which are digging the hole deeper with exorbitant interest rates.
- Prioritizing what obligations are most important: Your house is more significant than your department store credit card. It isn't always so evident, but you can make sure your early payments meet your most vital demands.
- Set a budget: This is where the discipline comes in. Once you have a decent notion of your monthly commitments, it is crucial to establish – and stay with – a strategy to fulfill them.
- Cut expenses: This is the more challenging component of keeping to a budget - avoiding superfluous spending.
- Identify spending habits: Do you need that third TV streaming service? Can you get by with adverts on your music streamer instead of that monthly fee? Some applications and websites

assist you to itemize the automatic monthly payments you have signed up for.

- Start paying off debt: Once you have arranged your money, stay with your strategy. When there is unexpected money, throw it against your debt rather than toss it away.
- Seek treatment for mental health: If all your efforts don't decrease your stress levels, or if all that attention on your debts instead raises your tension, don't attempt to cope with it alone.
- Pay now invoices quickly if possible: Adding to your debt burden is the reverse of decreasing your debt load.

Seek Support From Debtors Anonymous.

Seek Help from Mental Health and Financial Professionals

If financial troubles such as debt are generating stress, depression, and other mental health concerns, and mental health worries are making it harder to cope with money challenges - then, that is a spiral that you must find a method to slow down and stop.

Help is accessible in both areas. Some skilled specialists can give counseling and advice on debt, and there are professionals prepared with techniques to ease mental health difficulties.

For the latter, a recommended starting step is your doctor or another medical practitioner. They may be able to assist with minor mental health difficulties or recommend you to a therapist or psychiatrist equipped to treat more serious ones. The coping techniques they teach might aid when dealing with debt and other financial issues.

There are methods to acquire financial aid to address mental health concerns, so don't allow money to be a barrier to therapy.

One way to excellent mental health is to deal with stress-causing situations directly. There are several id debt-relief solutions available:

- Credit Counseling assists certified specialists who will help design a strategy to cope with your programs are frequently nonprofit and FREE of charge.
- Debt Management Programs are meant to consolidate credit card payments into one monthly payment with a reduced

interest rate. Such programs are provided by nonprofit credit counseling organizations.

- Debt Consolidation also combines unsecured debt like credit cards and pays them off by taking out a loan from a bank, credit union, or online lender to pay off the credit cards. You still must return the loan, but the interest rate should be substantially lower and you're just writing one check, instead of many payments.

Debt Settlement means paying less than what you owe. Achieving such is tough and time intensive. Lenders are not required to accept settlement proposals. It frequently takes 3-4 years to obtain a settlement with those that do. By that time, the late penalties and interest payments raise the debt you owe so substantially that a settlement may only be for 10 percent -20 percent of what you initially owed. And debt settlement is a blemish on your credit record that might drop your score by 100-200 points.

Bankruptcy protection comes in a few different packages, but it should only be regarded as a last resort when other choices have not been effective. If there is no possibility to repay your obligations in five years or less, bankruptcy can be the best alternative.

Whichever path you pursue toward debt reduction and resolution, one advantage is likely to be a decrease in the stress and worry that may have contributed to depression or more significant mental health difficulties. Lifting a load of debt from your shoulders will provide you with greater financial freedom and more discretionary cash to enjoy it with.

CHAPTER FOUR

GOOD DEBT Vs POOR DEBT

Good" debt is defined as money due for items that may assist develop wealth or boost income over time, such as college loans, mortgages, or business loans. "Bad" debt refers to items like credit cards or other consumer debt that do nothing to better your financial situation. These are oversimplifications.

Good debt can boost your net worth or enrich your life in a significant manner. Bad debt entails borrowing money to acquire fast depreciating assets or exclusively to consume

Examples of positive debt include taking out a mortgage, purchasing goods that save you time and money, buying critical items, and investing in yourself by borrowing for further education, or consolidating debt. Each may put you in a hole initially, but you'll be better off in the long term for having borrowed the money.

The one thing that keeps most Americans awake at night is neither a bumpy mattress nor being stalked by a nude Woody Harrelson in a dream.

It's the Big D - Debt.

And more than a year of living with COVID-19 hasn't helped. Some 64 percent of Americans regard money as a key cause of stress, according to the American Psychological Association; 52 percent blame the epidemic for affecting their financial status.

There's even a label for it: debt stress syndrome.

Americans are immersed in crimson ink. The Federal Reserve Bank of New York reported U.S. household debt topped $14.56 trillion in the fourth quarter of 2020, a $414 billion rise over the same time in 2019.

Credit-monitoring company Experian placed the average U.S. household debt by the end of 2020 at $92,727, a 10-year high.

So we're in danger, right? After all, Big D is menacing, a stress-inducing, panic-wreaking occurrence that may be a waking nightmare.

But wait. Tucked away in the Experian report is a modest reason for relief: Just as we've been taking on more debt, we've pushed down credit card balances by 14 percent — Experian calls it "historic" — and we've slashed home-equity line-of-credit debt, too.

The debt we've added? Home mortgages, student loans, and automotive loans. Which makes this as good a spot as any to address today's theme: Not all debt is created equal. Some merit all the trouble it creates.

What's The Difference?

A basic rule concerning debt is that if it raises your net worth or has future value, it's good debt.

If it doesn't accomplish that and you don't have funds to pay for it, it's terrible debt.

The second question is how do you realize you have too much debt?

There are broad signs, such as if your major source of money is selling your blood plasma. A widely acceptable indicator is your debt-to-income ratio.

Add all your monthly debt payments and divide them by your monthly gross income (not just your take-home pay) to obtain your debt-to-income ratio. For instance, if you have a $1,500 monthly mortgage, $200 vehicle payment, and pay $300 a month for credit cards and other payments, your monthly debt is $2,000.

If your gross monthly income is $4,000, that indicates your debt-to-income ratio is 50 percent.

It also implies you deserve your restless nights.

Anything above a 43 percent debt-to-income ratio is a warning signal to prospective lenders. Evidence shows that debtors with a greater percentage are more likely to have issues paying monthly payments. In most circumstances, you can't receive a mortgage if your ratio is over 43 percent.

That's unfortunate because guess what is arguably the best type of debt? Mortgages!

What's Considered Good Debt?

Good debt allows you to manage your finances more effectively, leverage your wealth, buy things you need, and handle □unforeseen emergencies.

Examples of positive debt are□ taking out a mortgage, purchasing goods that save you time and money, buying critical items, and investing in yourself by □borrowing for further education, or consolidating debt. Each may put you in a hole initially, but you'll be better off in the long term for having borrowed the money.

Taking out a Mortgage

The king of all debt is a mortgage. For one thing, you have to reside someplace. For another, you may as well reside someplace that improves in value practically every year.

After maintaining stability for much of the 20th century, home prices began a gradual ascent in 1968 until the mid-1990s, when they started climbing like the approach to Mt. Everest, culminating in November 2006. According to the Bureau of Labor Statistics, a home bought in 1967 for $100,000 would have cost about $681,000 in 2006. Housing values substantially outperformed inflation during the same era.

Yes, the real estate bubble burst in 2008 and momentarily made us question home ownership as the repository of American wealth. But look what's occurred since the gloomy bottom of the Great Recession in 2010: Houses are returning, big time, prices soaring 27.25 percent. In 2020 alone — in the middle of our nationwide coronavirus lockdown – property prices soared 10.8 percent, according to the Federal Housing Finance Agency.

The strength has remained consistent. Having shrugged off the worst consequences of irresponsible, predatory subprime lending, FHFA says home prices have increased every quarter since September 2011.

What's All This Imply In Actual Money?

If you purchase a property for $235,000 and it gains 3 percent a year, it will be worth $485,000 – more than twice what you bought it for – after your 30-year mortgage is paid off. If it gains 4 percent a year, the original $235,000 investment will be worth $649,000 or over three times the purchase price.

Now that's excellent debt.

Getting a Home Equity Loan or Line of Credit

Home equity loans and home-equity lines of credit are relatives of a mortgage. Borrowers receive a loan at a comparably low-interest rate using the equity — the value above the mortgage debt — of their property as security.

A lot of people obtain home-equity-based loans to pay off higher-interest obligations, such as credit cards. Some use it to make house renovations like solar panels that might save money on power costs and boost the value of their property.

The gamble isn't worry-free: Failure to keep up the payments might result in losing your property to foreclosure.

Getting a Student Loan

If you desire a decent education and need some assistance paying for it, you have plenty of company. The student loan sector is booming faster than Homer Simpson at a doughnut shop. The $1.6 trillion Americans hold in student loan debt ranks No. 2 on the extent of the nation's consumer debt, behind only mortgages. Student debt is more than twice credit card debt ($756.3 billion).

Borrowers also may be souring on the tradeoff of debt for higher education. In April, CNBC reported on a study of 1,000 30-something Millennials, 52 percent of whom think their loans weren't worth it.

Well. It's worth that if – and it's huge if – you are purchasing an education that will lead to a well-paying profession. Full-time employees over 25 with just high-school graduation had a median weekly salary of $789 in the middle of 2020, according to the Bureau of Labor Statistics.

The typical weekly pay for employees with at least a bachelor's degree was $1,416. But you must have the correct degree.

So with apologies to Waylon Jennings, moms let your kids grow up to be petroleum engineers ($92,300 a year after graduation), electrical engineers or computer scientists ($101,200), operations researchers ($78,400), or metallurgical engineers ($79,100), according to a 2020 PayScale study.
Anything in the so-called STEM disciplines (science, technology, engineering, and mathematics) offers tremendous income potential. On the opposite hand, you could never pay off your student debt if you study liberal arts. A psychology degree begins at around ally$42,000 a year when they join the real world.
If your ambition is to major in photography arts or philosophy or human development, your buddies may advise you to pursue it. Your financial adviser will not.

Small Business Loan

If you want to become very, really wealthy, your chances are significantly greater if you create your ark for yourself. Entrepreneurism is all the rage, and ideas for successful small enterprises abound. But have a strategy, and maybe some personal supporters. Small company loans are difficult to secure because they are riskier to the lender.
Almost one-third of small firms fail to survive their first two years, according to the Small Business Administration. But if you have the desire, intelligence and luck, borrowing money to start your own company might be the finest investment you'll ever make. What Is Bad Debt?
Spotting bad debt isn't all that tough. If it loses value the instant you acquire possession, it's bad debt. Unfortunately, it characterizes many of life's essential requirements, including clothing, autos, and that bad boy 80-inch UHD TV you need to watch NFL games.
If you can't pay cash for them, you should at least consider settling with off-brand clothing, a lightly preowned automobile, and 54-inch TV.
Here are instances of bad debt.

Credit Cards

Plastic may harm your financial health, and interest rates are the silent killer. Figuring them out is complicated, and that's great for credit card companies. If customers realize how much they truly pay for the pleasure of using a card, they'd attack the houses of every card company president.

Remember that 80-inch UHD TV? Say you were very, very fortunate and bought one at an open-box sale for $1,200, and you placed on your Visa with the 18.9 percent interest rate.

If you paid $60 a month (which would be more than the minimum necessary), it would take 63 months to pay off and cost a total of $1,676.98. That's a steep charge to see Trevor Lawrence in ultra-high definition.

U.S. families holding credit card debt from month to month crept up to 43 percent in 2020, from 37 percent in 2019. At the same time, average credit card debt per borrower decreased by 12 percent, to $5,111 (from $5,835).

That's a promising trend, but if you are among those utilizing more than 30 percent of available credit, your credit score is likely to suffer. That implies higher interest rates when you seek a loan or new credit.

Payday Loans

As awful as credit cards are, payday loans are 10 to 15 times worse. You obtain short-term funding to help you through a catastrophe. In return, you post-date a check, hoping you can pay off the debt when your next paycheck comes (usually two weeks) (typically two weeks).

It's fast and simple, but the loan costs run from $15 to $30 for every $100 borrowed. A typical two-week payday loan with a $15-per-$100 cost corresponds to an annual percentage rate of 400 percent. If it doesn't trigger nausea, ignore the gastroenterologist; you need to see a psychologist (they can use the business) (they can use the business).

Automobile Loans

Financing an automobile normally is considered bad debt since, unless it's a 1966 Mustang or some other collector, car prices decrease 20 percent less than a half-mile off the lot.
On the other hand, automotive loan rates are comparably cheap (1.4 percent -2.5 percent for new with excellent credit; 2.5 percent and above for used), and if you need a car to drive to work, well, a man or gal needs to make a livelihood.
The most financially wise strategy is to avoid splurging on a Mercedes when a Hyundai would suffice. If you want ultimately to purchase an SL 550 Roadster, you'll need what debt you have to be good, so pay this loan off on schedule.

CHAPTER FIVE

9 REASONS DEBT IS BAD FOR YOU

A little debt won't harm, will it? That's how it begins. You make a modest purchase on your credit card, and suddenly, before you know it, you're hundreds of dollars in debt. But what precisely is wrong with having a little—or a lot—of debt? To start with, here are nine difficulties debt may create in your life.

1. Debt Encourages You to Spend More Than You Can Afford.

There's something about the debt that tempts you to keep spending even when you can't make the payments. Part of the attractiveness of debt is the fact that you may enjoy the emotional high from receiving new items immediately, without having to cope with the immediate sorrow of parting with money. It might seem like you're receiving something for nothing. But someday, that spending will come up with you, and it won't feel so nice then.

2. **Debt Costs Money.**

Debt seems free while you're swiping your card or signing loan paperwork, but this is an illusion. In general, you pay a price for the debt you generate. That fee comes in the shape of interest. The greater the interest rate, the more you'll end up paying for your loan. Also, the longer it takes you to pay off and the bigger your debt burden, the more interest you'll pay.

The sole exception is an interest-free loan or zero percent APR credit card offer, but even it has a limit and may be lost if you fail on your payments.

3. **Debt Borrows From Your Future Income**

Any time you take out a loan or charge anything on your credit card, you're borrowing from the money you intend to earn in the future. Do you want to waste your money paying for something you've already used up and don't receive any value from anymore? You never know what changes may happen in your income, therefore it's wiser not to mortgage your future.

4. High-Interest Debt Causes You to Pay More Than the Item Cost.

If you purchase a $2,000 living room set on your credit card at 11 percent and simply make the minimum payment, you'll wind up spending more than $3,600 by the time you entirely pay off the loan. That's $1,600 more than the furniture cost. Even if you were to boost your monthly payment to $100 and pay off the amount, you'd still pay close to $220 more than the cost of the furnishings. On the other hand, you may save away $150 a month for 14 months and pay in full at no additional expense.

5. Debt Keeps You from Reaching Your Financial Goals.

Monthly debt payments restrict the amount of money you have to spend on other things—not only retirement, but the vacation you always wanted to take or Christmas gifts for your family. The more debt you incur, the greater your monthly payments will be, and the less you have to spend on everything else.

6. Debt Can Keep You from Owning a Home

Credit card, vehicle, and student loan debt are all examined when you apply for a house loan. If your existing debt payments are too high, you may be turned down for a home loan. In most circumstances, your total monthly loan payments can't take up more than 43 percent of your income if you intend to acquire a mortgage. Many lenders want that number to be even lower. That means you'll be stuck renting or paying on your present mortgage until you pay off some of your other debt.

7. Debt Can Lead to Stress and Serious Medical Problems.

When you have debt, it's hard not to worry about how you're going to make your payments or how you'll refrain from taking on additional debt to make ends meet. The stress from debt may lead to minor to severe health issues like ulcers, headaches, depression, and even heart attacks. 2 The further you sink into debt, the more probable it is that you may experience health difficulties.

8. Debt Can Hurt Your Marriage.

Debt puts undue strain on the household's finances and produces a lack of financial stability for your spouse and your children. When both couples feel stressed, it may cause conflicts over spending patterns, who is producing more debt, and how much debt is too much. These disagreements might grow and lead to a collapse in the marriage.

9. Debt Hurts Your Credit Score

Part of your credit score—30 percent to be exact—is dependent on the amount of debt you have. The more debt you have relative to your credit limits and initial loan sums, the worse your credit score will be. Even if you're not shopping for a credit card or loan, your credit score influences your life and the cost of other goods and services, such as auto insurance

CHAPTER SIX

6 STRATEGIES TO GET OUT OF DEBT

Getting out of debt isn't simple. Sometimes it takes all you have to keep up with monthly expenses and save for a rainy day, much alone make the minimum monthly payments on your credit card. Fortunately, there are many methods to get out of debt that won't make you unhappy. Here are some of the finest techniques to become debt free.

What's The Average Debt Per Person?

According to the 2019 Consumer Debt Study from Experian, the typical American had $90,460 in debt in 2018. This statistic comprises mortgages, credit card debt, vehicle loans, personal loans, and school loans.
Here's how it breaks down by generation:

Age group	Average debt load
Gen Z (18-23)	$9,593
Millennials (24-39)	$78,396
Gen X (40-55)	$135,841
Baby boomers (56-74)	$96,984

HOW DEBT MAY SEVERELY AFFECT YOUR LIFE

Being in debt might make applying for other loans more challenging. For example, if you want to purchase a home, most lenders demand that you have a debt-to-income (DTI) ratio of 43 percent or less, including future mortgage payments.
The DTI ratio is established by summing up your existing monthly loan payments and dividing them by your monthly gross income. Let's assume you have a $300 student loan payment, a $500 vehicle loan payment, and a $200 minimum credit card payment. Your monthly gross income is $3,750, which makes your DTI 26.67 percent. In this situation, the highest mortgage payment you would qualify for is $612.50. Depending on your region, it might be extremely hard to locate a property within that price range.
If your DTI already surpasses 43 percent without a mortgage payment, you may find it hard to qualify for a mortgage. Having too

much debt might also make it tougher to invest for retirement, your child's college tuition, or other ambitions.

Additionally, if you work in law enforcement, financial services, or the military, your employer may run a credit check when you apply. You may be rejected if you have too much debt since a fragile financial state puts you at a statistically greater risk for taking bribes.

Organize all of your debt and bills

Before you can develop a debt paydown plan, you need to gather a list of all of your current expenses and debts. Go through your bank and credit card accounts for the previous six months and jot down all the regular loans, invoices, and other fixed costs.

Your list should contain the monthly payment, total debt, interest rate, period, and any other pertinent facts. For example, you should note whether any of the loans are presently in deferral or on a special repayment plan.

Make sure you read your credit report from all three credit agencies. Some lenders don't record credit activity with all three, so if you just check one or two you may be missing vital information.

Strategies to get out of debt

If you're ready to get out of debt, start with the following steps.

1. Pay more than the minimum payment

Go over your budget and determine how much more you can spend on your debt. Paying more than the minimum can save you money on interest and help you get out of debt quicker.

Let's imagine you have a $15,000 debt on a credit card with 17 percent APR and a $450 minimum payment. If you merely make the minimal payment, it will take you approximately four years to repay the remainder. You'll pay around $5,500 in total interest.

If you paid $550 a month, or $100 more than the minimum, you could repay the loan in less than three years and pay just $4,100 in total interest. To understand more, consider utilizing a credit card payment calculator.

2. Try the debt snowball

If you're paying more than the minimum payment, you may also attempt the debt snowball approach for debt reduction. This debt repayment plan urges you to make the minimum payment on all your debts except for the lowest one, which you'll pay as much as you can toward. By "snowballing" payments toward your lowest debt, you'll eradicate it fast and move on to the next smallest obligation while making minimum payments on the others.

Let's imagine you have a $5,000 credit card bill, a $1,000 vehicle loan, and $10,000 in school loans. With the debt snowball strategy, you would concentrate on paying off the vehicle loan first, since it has the lowest overall sum.

The debt snowball approach may help drive you to concentrate on one debt at a time instead of numerous, helping you create momentum and remain on track. The only time you should ignore the debt snowball approach as an option is if you have a payday loan or a title loan. These loans normally have substantially higher interest rates, from 300 percent to 400 percent APR on average, and should be paid off as quickly as feasible.

3. Refinance debt

Refinancing debt to a lower interest rate may save you hundreds in interest and help you repay debt quicker. You may refinance mortgages, vehicle loans, personal loans, and school loans.

One option to achieve this is with a debt consolidation loan, which is a personal loan that may come with cheaper interest rates than your previous loans. If you have credit card debt, you may also consider moving the amount to a balance transfer card. These cards carry 0 percent APR for a certain period generally between six to 18 months.

4. Commit windfalls to debt

When you receive a tax return or stimulus check, put the money to your debts instead of storing it in your bank account or indulging in yourself. You may elect to devote the full windfall or divide it 50-50 between debt and something pleasurable, like a future trip or costly supper.

Other unexpected windfalls, such as instances, job bonuses, and financial gifts, may also be utilized to pay off debts quicker. Remember, every little amount helps while working towards your debt-payoff objectives.

5. Settle for less than you owe

You may also phone creditors and negotiate a settlement of your obligations, generally for a lot less than you owe. While it's feasible to take care of this yourself, a variety of third-party firms also provide debt settlement services for a cost.

While paying less than you owe and fleeing past obligations may sound wise, the Federal Trade Commission does note certain concerns. For instance, some debt settlement organizations require you to suspend making payments on your obligations while you're negotiating better terms, which may adversely damage your credit score.

6. Re-examine your budget

There are two methods to pay off your debts quickly — earn more or spend less. It may not be realistic to take up a part-time job or side business, but you may make modifications to your budget.

Start by taking a look at each item in your spending plan and sorting them depending on their degree of priority. Classify each line item as a necessity or desire, and highlight costs that may be decreased or fully eliminated. Make the necessary modifications to your budget, and use the money you free up to pay more on your debts each month.

CHAPTER SEVEN

11 MISTAKES TO AVOID WHEN PAYING OFF DEBT

There are three realities about debt:

- Getting into it may be enjoyable.
- Getting out of it is not.

- It's worth that effort.

That's because being in debt is like living beneath a gloomy cloud. Getting out of debt may be life-altering. Millions of people have done it, so why not join them?

But remember that it means more than paying off credit cards. It requires altering your spending patterns, learning how to budget, monitoring your costs, prioritizing debts, generating emergency and retirement accounts, and knowing where to obtain assistance.

It's a complicated procedure, and it's easy to make errors along the way. Here are some of the key ones you'll want to avoid.

Mistake 1: Not adjusting your spending habits.

Is your handbag or wallet on autopilot? Do you visit Starbucks every morning? Go food shopping without a list? Feel an insatiable need to get the newest iPhone? Pick up supper at Applebee's on the way home from work?

Such habits make your life easy, convenient, and cool. They also enable money to be unnecessarily drained from your bank account.

Remedy: Get off autopilot. Consider how much you may save by modifying your habit.

- Find cheaper options. Spending $4.95 a day for a Caffe Mocha? That's $99 a month if you constantly stop on the way to work.
- Make a shopping list before heading to the grocery store and stick to it.
- Try to exist without the newest iPhone and three or four streaming services.
- Eat in more frequently.
- The overspending instances are only symptoms. To dig out the issue, consider what you were thinking about when you purchased those products.

The answer is probably "nothing." You were on autopilot. Turn it off, track your spending and turn on the savings.

Mistake 2: Trying to get out of debt alone.

It can be done, but it can also be more simply done. All you need is a little assistance, however, asking for aid suggests you have a problem. Some individuals don't want friends or family to know that.

Remedy: Get free and private assistance. It's offered through nonprofit credit counseling services, which are staffed by experienced and qualified counselors.

They may propose debt-relief measures including debt management programs, credit consolidation, debt settlement, or even bankruptcy if your financial illnesses demand severe treatment. Counselors can also construct a budget and assist you in learning how to remain out of debt for good.

Mistake 3: Signing up for an Illegitimate Debt Relief Program .

Debt reduction solutions may you out of your financial hole. Just remember that digging software. If software looks too simple to be true, it usually is.

Remedy: Don't trust in debt alleviation magic. Debt relief fraudsters will offer exaggerated promises and collect unnecessary costs. So, how can you pick a decent debt relief company?

Keep in mind that there is no fast remedy. Debt-relief programs often take 3-5 years, so be patient. Also, be willing to dig yourself out. If an agency promises you won't need to, it's shoveling malarkey.

Mistake 4: Not developing a reasonable budget.

At the risk of overstating things, getting out of debt is like going to battle. If you attempt to wing it, you'll probably end up waving the white flag.

Remedy: Come up with a realistic combat strategy. It will handle basics including shelter, food, transportation, health care, insurance, and education. It will also generate space for you to pay off your debt.

An excellent place to start is by getting rid of your credit cards. We'll stop now to let Visa junkies complete their spasms. You'll think twice if you have to spend cash for stuff like eating out, movies, leather boots, and electrical gizmos.

Mistake 5: Trying to pay off numerous debts at once.

There are payments you must pay each month, such as mortgages, vehicle loans, and electricity. Then there are debts you may pay a fraction of, like credit cards. People frequently strive to address each of those each month. Bad move.

Remedy: Pay the most costly one off first. That's the bill with the highest interest rate. It makes more logical sense to pay $100 toward a loan with 18 percent interest, than $50 toward that debt and $50 toward the debt with a 6 percent interest rate. Take care of the higher-interest debt first, then work your way down.

Mistake 6: Closing accounts after they are paid off.

Once you've finally paid off a credit card, two cravings strike. You want to rejoice, and you want to terminate the account - bury that sucker once and for all.

Follow through with the initial desire. The second one will be your financial recovery.

Remedy: Don't cancel the account. It seems paradoxical, but it's preferable to leave unused credit cards open. Credit scoring models reward customers for having long-standing credit accounts and for utilizing just a tiny fraction of their credit limit. Unless the card has a hefty annual charge, retain it. Just don't use it.

Mistake 7: Borrowing from or discontinuing payments to a 401(k)

A lot of folks have one lump of money they could utilize to pay off debt - their retirement savings. That's one approach to address the issue, but you have to consider the long-term and ask yourself, "Do I want to die in old age with a McDonald's uniform on?"

Remedy: Don't raid your retirement fund or take out a 401(k) loan to pay off today's bills. First, there are frequently significant financial penalties if you withdraw money early. Second, many firms at least partly match your retirement contributions. That's free money.

Third, understand how retirement income appreciates. The sooner you start donating, the more time it will have to develop. If feasible, contribute 5 percent to 10 percent of your income for your retirement. If that's not doable, fine. Just don't raid your retirement.

Your golden years aren't intended to be spent working at the Golden Arches.

Mistake 8: Not putting away emergency funds.

About 56 percent of Americans didn't have $1,000 in savings to compensate for an emergency in January of 2022, according to a Bankrate survey. Are you ready if your vehicle breaks down or your roof springs a leak or your dog attacks the neighbor and you need a lawyer?

Remedy: Get prepared. You need 3-6 months of spending in an emergency fund. It may take a while but make it part of your budget. Put 5 percent of your money toward covering life's unanticipated issues. If nothing else, you'll probably sleep a lot better.

Mistake 9: Not checking your credit report is accurate.

About 34 percent of Americans detected at least one inaccuracy on their credit reports, according to a 2021 survey by Consumer Reports. You might find yourself paying for someone else's error if you don't submit a credit dispute.

Remedy: Check your credit records. The three main credit reporting agencies — Equifax, Experian, and TransUnion – provide you with one free credit report a year. Look for inaccurate delinquencies and/or balances that harm your credit score and make it tougher to secure a loan.

Mistake 10: Not prioritizing your debt.

Unlike the federal government, individual Americans can't simply keep building up debt as though it would never come crashing back down on them. Due to interest rates, your financial hole is simply going to become worse if you ignore it.

Remedy: Focus on the issue, and the solution. One approach to get focused is to grab a piece of paper the size of a credit card and write down five debts you wish to get rid of. Tape it to your credit card. Every time you go for that card, you'll be reminded that you're adding, not subtracting to the issue.

As for remedies, the easiest is to develop a strategy, set a budget, and adhere to it. If you need assistance, millions of Americans have found relief by combining their debts into one monthly payment via a debt management program.

Mistake 11: Not moving your debt to better credit cards.

Credit cards are not inherently wicked. Truth is, they're pretty helpful when utilized correctly. Imagine you owe $4,000 on a credit card with a 15.99 interest rate. If you convert it to a card with a 0 percentage of 18 months and pay $225 a month, you'd save $600 interest.

Remedy: Apply for a balance transfer credit card with a 0 percent or extremely low introductory interest rate and transfer your previous credit card debt to the new card.

If you can qualify, these cards may give you the breathing space you need to fight your credit card load. Just remember, an 's an "introductory" rate. When it expires, it will rise. If you don't pay it off in the allocated period, you might finish yourself in worse trouble than you began.

NOW YOU KNOW ERRORS TO AVOID. WHAT'S NEXT?

Here are a few steps to get you started. Some repeat what you've previously learned, but they are worth hammering home.

- Check your budget -
- There always are places where you may chop a few dollars free and produce additional income to apply to the debt. One fewer night dining out (at least $20 saved). Take your lunch to work every day (at least $20 saved). Watch the movie or athletic event at home (at least $20 saved). Skip Happy Hour ($20 saved).
- Bury your credit card -

That's what got you in trouble. Keep one in your wallet for real emergencies. Pay for everything else in cash. It's a LOT more difficult to give up a $100 note that it is a credit card. Impulse shopping nearly vanishes when you're young.

- Go shopping with a list –

A grocery store or shopping mall is a hazardous place when all you take is a credit card. Make a list of things you desire. Only purchase what is on the list. Get in, get out. And never go grocery shopping while you're hungry. Even Spam seems appetizing on an empty stomach.

- Share the cost —

Roommates lower the cost of everything in half, maybe more, if they're truly thrifty. You pay less on rent, less on food, less on utilities, less on cable, and even less on transportation. In most circumstances, the savings gained by dividing expenditures will be enough to dramatically decrease your debt by itself.

- Take one more look around the home -

Do you 00 a month's worth of cable TV? Does spending $50-$75 for a game of golf make sense? Can you mow the yard and clean the home yourself? How about exercising without a gym membership? All those things are lovely to have ... if you're not in debt. Dump them till you've paid off the last of your credit cards.

- Get some assistance —

If you are still flummoxed by debt, visit a nonprofit credit counseling firm online and go through one of their free credit counseling sessions. They assist you sort out your issue; they help you put up a manageable budget, and they advise you on which debt-relief solution best matches your condition. The counselors are qualified and certified. And, best of all, it's FREE!

How to Pay Off Debt Faster

All that belt-tightening may not seem like fun, but you can hasten your financial comeback. These measures should also enable you to reward yourself with an occasional night out or a game of golf.

- Generate more money —

There were approximately 5 million more job opportunities than available employees in January 2022, according to the Bureau of

Labor Statistics. Getting a second job, even if it's only a few hours a week, maybe a hassle, but it will be time well spent.

- Pay all payments on time —

You're merely throwing away money when you're late paying monthly expenses. Late fines are a gold mine for credit card companies, landlords, and banks. They don't have to perform any more labor to receive extra money. Don't give away your money.

- Garage sale, anyone? –

Nearly everyone has outdated TVs, laptops, gym equipment, furniture, and clothing they just don't use anymore. Let someone pay you to take away your rubbish.

- Unbudgeted income —

You may obtain a tax return or payout from an estate you never planned. Forget about a weekend trip. Spend the money towards eliminating debt.

- Ask for a rate reduction -

If you haven't looked at the interest rates you're paying, particularly on credit cards, have a look at your account and find out. If you have been a regular, on-time payment, your card company will want to maintain your business. Tell them they can, if they decrease your interest rate to the lowest levels. This is one situation where "Ask and you shall receive," should truly work.

- Ask for a raise —

Businesses have been rich with money for a long, but the latest tax cuts should make their bottom lines much greater. Unemployment is at its lowest level. The combination implies there may never be a better time to earn a raise. The worst that may happen is you receive another "No!"

www.ingramcontent.com/pod-product-compliance
Lightning Source LLC
LaVergne TN
LVHW080558160826
845677LV00010B/1905
9798846105553